SUMMER PROMISES

and other poems

Sanil Sachar is a young poet born in New Delhi. He is currently studying for a degree in sport business management at Sheffield Hallam University, South Yorkshire, United Kingdom. In his free time, he loves penning down his thoughts and articulating his everyday experiences in the form of verse.

Praise for the book

'This book is a diary of living life in all its simplicity and immediacy. It is about growing to know things in the process of growing up with things. It leaves nothing to be desired and no desire to be left unfulfilled. Sanil complains and yet comes to terms. He feels and yet leaves nothing to be felt. Through his direct style, he expresses what he feels, without inhibition or restraint. He keeps setting things right as they seem to go wrong, for the world and for himself.'

—Muzaffar Ali

SUMMER PROMISES

and other poems

Sanil Sachar

RUPA

Published by
Rupa Publications India Pvt. Ltd 2013
7/16, Ansari Road, Daryaganj
New Delhi 110002

Sales centres:
Allahabad Bengaluru Chennai
Hyderabad Jaipur Kathmandu
Kolkata Mumbai

Copyright © Sanil Sachar 2013

All rights reserved.
No part of this publication may be reproduced, transmitted, or stored in a retrieval system, in any form or by any means, electronic, mechanical, photocopying, recording or otherwise, without the prior permission of the publisher.

ISBN: 978-81-291-2371-8

10 9 8 7 6 5 4 3 2 1

The moral right of the author has been asserted.

Typeset in GoudyOldStyle BT 10.5/15

This book is sold subject to the condition that it shall not, by way of trade or otherwise, be lent, resold, hired out, or otherwise circulated, without the publisher's prior consent, in any form of binding or cover other than that in which it is published.

For everyone, who made it possible
for this dream to turn into reality

Contents

Preface

Here I am, miles away from home, away from my loved ones, amidst a whole new set of friends, living a completely different life. But one constant companion that has been by my side, apart from my loved ones, is poetry.

Poetry is a box full of memories which I glance through every once in a while and it brings a smile to my face. I never thought that I would write someday. Sports had been my passion since I joined school. I followed my passion and landed in a boarding school in England. Along with the realisation of being thousands of miles away from my loved ones, I gained more time to myself–and here is where my interest in poetry developed. These years of being away from home have made me realise a lot more about myself and the experiences that life has offered me have helped me in penning down my thoughts on paper.

The poems in this book are the experiences that have got me this far. I thank you all for being a part of my journey, and wish you all the luck for yours.

Sanil

Vision

Everything that comes your way
Is what you want and say
Vision is the key
Your thoughts are what you see
Impossible is only a word in the dictionary
But nothing can stop a visionary

Nothing stays on forever
Everything has its time
Don't delay your actions
It'll slow down your climb

Don't let your thoughts have a roof
Let sky be the limit
And result of your success be the proof

Haters appear when success is close
Don't let them affect your pace
They are a symbol that you're the one leading the race

Every burden is a sign
Don't let it bring you down
Because once you tackle it, everything will be fine
And your smile will get rid of the frown

Be willing to die
If you want to win a fight
Nobody is born a winner
You have to earn the right

The master of your faith
The captain of your soul
Be the only person
Standing in front of you and your goal

The Unnoticed Hero

Under all that dust and sweat
I too was a youngster living in threat
But people seem to get me wrong
Nobody ever called me strong

Is this enough proof for you?
Have I done enough to get my message through?
While you lay there safe in your bed
Here I am six feet under the ground, buried, dead

Was I just another example of corruption?
If I was corrupt
I wouldn't have saved you by dying in this eruption
I'm sorry mom and dad but I couldn't stay any longer
I wish I was stronger

Under those mud piles and sleeping on those hard terrains
Something pulled me back, as if I was tied back by chains
Maybe it was to prove all those doubters wrong
Maybe it was me reassuring myself that this is where I belong

I never wondered what else I could have done
My whole life was about dodging bullets and reloading my gun

Here I am hung up on the wall
Along with my mates who took the fall
To serve my country was my primary aim
Hope I'm the last one to be put up in frame

ᔕ

Tranquil Paradise

It's 6:30 a.m., the city is asleep
I'm sitting outside, watching the sunrise
Wondering if this is reality
Or if my alarm will beep

It seems like a new world
One with no corruption and nothing known as crime
If I had a remote
I'd pause this moment and keep reliving this time

No sight of pollution, no sound of honking cars
Peace and tranquillity be the only ingredients
While the sun takes over its shift from the stars

Everything seems too surreal to be true
This world doesn't seem like the havoc we are a part of
However much I hope for it to

We should all be owls and stay up till the early morn
So we can be a part of this tranquil paradise
And forget the sound of speeding cars or their loud horn

The clock strikes seven and with the hour
The world doesn't seem the same
People wake up for work

Everything is noisy and chaotic
Only making me realise
It's us who are to blame

∽

Unanswered Questions

Why do we come here?
Where do we go?
Why does it all stop like an old radio?

What are we supposed to do?
Why can't we stay?
Why does it all end like we were in a play?

Why aren't you here?
More importantly, where are you?
Am I speaking to anyone?
Is someone listening to me?

I've got questions but I'm naive
I watch television
And I know this world is hard to survive

I keep hearing about this ring
I think it starts with suffer
I've heard once you wear it
It only makes life tougher

I'm now no longer naive
And I seem to understand how to survive
Thank you for all that I have
But I'm still waiting for those answers to arrive

I can drive now
So can you give me your post code?
I'll reach you somehow
I just need to get rid of this entire load

It's a bit unfair, don't you think?
How our lives alter with every blink
Everything changes
Nothing stays the same
You and your friends can't take our lives to be a game

I'm grateful for what you've given me
But if the answers are kept in a safe
All I'm asking for is the key
Because by the end of the day
We all have the right to know
Why we come here
If we have to go

ᔕ

A Box Full of Memories

Look at this picture, is that me?
Sitting in the sand, building castles
With an expression full of joy and naivety

I look at this picture and look at myself, where I stand
Seems like all that youth got washed away with the sand

I flip through another album
I am entering school for the first time
Oblivious to what lies ahead of me
Yet my expression suggests this moment to be sublime

There I am with my football team
All the matches and practise sessions
Flow through my head like a stream
We may not have won most of our games
But nothing will make me forget any of their names

If these pictures ever take me back to those days
There won't be a moment I'd want to erase
I glimpse through this box of memories every once in a while
Because those times never fail to make me smile

They are a time machine
Taking my life in a flashback

From joy to nostalgia
Like a roller coaster to my journey from a new born
To a teenager at nineteen

I look in the mirror and see myself today
These pictures always help me from going astray
I walk out of the door to be who I want to be
So, each time I flip through a new album
I'll remember a fond memory

An Unwanted Feeling

Why! Why did this happen to me?
What have I done, for this to be?
These are words most of us say
For the smallest of issues that come our way
Whether it's failing a test
Or not getting enough rest
At whining we all are the best

But problems aren't as big as they seem
Biggest obstacles vanish like steam
Be the person Bob Marley wanted us to be
To be happy

Whenever you feel down
Look around you
Because even after a stormy night the sky turns blue

Regret is an unwanted feeling
We worry although nothing can be done
It's like an evil miniature living within us
Without paying rent

Problems aren't as big as they seem
We have to beat our troubles to reach our dream

∽

2012 Summer!

That time of the year has almost begun
When we put aside all the work we have done
Lay back and enjoy our reservation with the sun

It's that time of the year
When the only mode we know is calm
Wake up when we want to
And forget the use of an alarm

The time of the year
When the only feeling is excitement
And 'what's the plan for tonight?'
Is all we want to hear

So lock up all your work
And push away all your worries
Let's just create good memories

Enjoying the sun and lazing around is all I have planned
Work and assignments
Ha! They are all banned

Time flies when you're having fun
Let this summer be something out of a dream
Live it up from midnight till the rise of the sun

So when you look back
It should feel like a home run

So get ready for a celebration bigger than any hummer
Because this isn't just any time of the year
It's 2012 Summer!

∽

Leave Me Alone

Leave me alone now
I have an exam in finance
Unless you teach me all the ratios somehow
Logout yourself because you don't stand a chance

You may not have an option to dislike
But it's times like these I wish you would take a hike
I'm not in the mood for anymore commenting
Let my books be the only quotes I read
And stop with all this tormenting

If I could justify a reason for my poor grade
Facebook, you'd top the list
I don't 'like' you at exam time
I wish you'd fade away in mist

How do you suddenly get of so much interest
When I open a book to learn for a test?
If you cause so much failure and havoc
Why aren't you classed as a drug?
If you were a disease
You'd be the worst bug

If stalking profiles were a part of our course
Facebook, you'd be my revision's best source

But for now you're every student's worst addiction
At this time you should be the biggest restriction

I wish I could go up to my examiner
And give this justification
Sir, the only reason I couldn't study
Was because of my notifications
My friend's status caused a debate
I was studying at first but then he tagged me
And I became the bait

My three hours of revision now include
Two hours of stalking people on Facebook
And the rest realising I'm screwed

You Facebook, are like marmalade
You are either liked or completely despised
So, I don't know with what aid
But you've got to get me a good grade

∽

Another Day Gone By

Another day has gone away
I think of all I've done
While I lay

Why haven't I reached my aim?
Why haven't I got what I want to claim?
How did Zuckerberg and Messi get the fame?
What all did they do to become who they became?

We all have ambitions
Our vision of something we want to do
An aim to reach the highest positions
A thought so prominent in us
Like an invisible tattoo

Another day has gone away
I'm still in the same place where I lay
It's like running on a treadmill
I can feel myself moving forward but in reality
I'm at the same place still

I don't understand why it's taking so long
These dreams of mine run through my head
Like my favourite song

What did they do to get where they are?
We only know them now
But they know the struggles they had to do to get this far

Yet another day has gone by
I'm finally realizing the method I need to apply
The finish line is still far away
But by putting my thoughts into actions
I can shorten this delay

∽

Nineteen to Twenteen

There are mud trails on the floor
Clothes scattered all over the bed
Responsibility isn't a book that has been read
Oh teenage years, you are a part of my life I'll always adore!

How I'll miss acting like a young child
Getting away with stupidity was a privilege
Along with the right to go completely wild

No more delegation of your own work
And being backed with the excuse of being a teenager
It's time to learn how to solely tackle any potential danger

Maybe thirteen to nineteen isn't enough time
To enjoy my years as a teen
So when the clock strikes 12 on the sixteen
Refer to me as turning twenteen

Age is merely a number that tags along with us
It's up to us to let this number make a difference
Or stay young without making a fuss

As I get out of my teens
With being an adult as the next ship to sail
I'll try and stay a teen forever
And if in doubt
I'll trace back to who I was via those mud trails

Dear Haters

So what if you are bigger than me
Stronger than me
Faster than me
Look in the mirror
You're you, not me

I may not have sharp ears
But I hear everything you say
And every time you talk behind my back
I think you need to try harder
This bitching of yours isn't affecting me in any way

Oh wait! You're richer than me?
Didn't know all that you've done
Wait, are you Richard Branson?
Ha! I knew you're just a regular hater
All talk, no walk
And you thought you have the right to mock?

You want to compete?
You want to have something to talk about?
Go pick on someone you can actually beat!

I can talk too
I can make up stories just like you

But I don't have the time
Because there's lot I want to do

This is to all you haters
You can keep on talking
It's you who are helping me get to where I want to be
You do the talking, I'll do the walking
I'm not you, I'm me

∽

2012

It's going to blow up
We'll all be dead
Wait, you don't know what's up?
The world is going to end
At least that's what the Mayans said

What's your plan till the end date?
Are you going to live your life to the fullest?
Or are you going to sit back, relax and wait?

To me, this myth doesn't make sense
I don't mean to be harsh
Mayans, you may know more than me
So, no offence

Thank you for giving us a deadline
Now I have a reason to do all that I want to
And if I mess up
I'll blame you for giving us this closing time

So, will you use this myth as an excuse to quit?
Or will it be a reason to accomplish all that you want to?
So, just in case the Mayans are correct
You'll be happy about where you sit

∽

My Incomplete Affair...

They say, you don't think much when you're young
And your decisions are completely honest and true
I'll cut to the chase
This middle school crush
Turned into a high school phase over you

If we had a story
I'm sure it would be a hit that no one would want to miss
We started as strangers
Turned into friends
And now strangers is back to where it is

It's true what goes around
Comes back around
But if I had a time machine
I think we both know where I'll be bound

Do I regret not taking the chance?
Do I regret not wanting things to advance?
At times I do
But would life still be the same if I did?
I can't answer that and neither can you

I wonder if you're glad things ended up this way
I wonder if you remember those long hours

In the field between lessons
And how you always got me to stay

I'm glad I didn't take the chance
I'm hoping this risk of mine will benefit in the long run
Football, my love for you will always be young
Thank you for all the times we've shared
But we still have a lot undone

∽

Enjoy the Ride

I'll pen down some words and forget everything sad
And shine some wisdom like a preacher
Instead of being a nineteen-year-old lad

I know I'm not experienced
To write down a story on myself
I'll just add this poem with the rest on my shelf
I've not done much till now
And I'm not promising any wonders to come
Don't judge me on who I am and what all I've done

Forget all your worries and all the crime that surrounds us
How to enjoy this ride is all I'd like to discuss
I'll keep this simple and easy
Let this poem be a breather
From your hectic lives, from me

This life is yours and nobody can have it
The only thing certain in your life is you
Don't let anyone grab it

Make mistakes, they become the best stories to tell
Don't keep any thoughts in your head
This world is huge
Shout out your thoughts
It's worth the yell

Be nice to others, in doing so, there is no shame
It's better than messing with the wrong person
And ending up in pain

Don't think too much, I know I won't
The best form of not worrying is when you don't

All in all, this life is a ride
So sit and enjoy it with all those you love by your side
One ride is all we get
Make this life one you never forget

∽

Being Rich

Being rich isn't what it seems
Money can't buy you all your dreams
As a child we dream of the wildest things
But with time, money makes the rich greedy
And wealth turns into their everything

The rich could invest in buying some sense
Instead of spending loads on brands
To secure the first place in this materialistic land

People are funny
Spending money they haven't earned
To buy things they don't need
To impress people they don't like

Everyone has their price
Don't act like you don't know what I'm on about
Because with the right ingredients
Even sugar can turn into spice

Money may buy power
And it can make any thought seem sublime
But nobody is rich enough in this world
To buy happiness all the time

Time is money and money is time
I've heard this line in many songs
But have never understood the rhyme
Oh well! I may need to employ a professional to explain this
Damn! I guess money does control this world
Only if there was no such monstrosity
This world would be a bliss

∽

Illusion or Reality?

Ever wondered that all this is a dream?
You wake up and these years
Haven't really gone as it seems

You're back to being naive and young
The answers to what the future has laid out for you
Are at the tip of your tongue

Would you be glad you were given this preview?
Would you carry on the same way?
Or would you learn from the trailer
And start completely anew?

Ever had the feeling where you've done something
And it feels unreal?
You wish you aren't dreaming
Because this feeling of achievement is surreal

Ever wondered that all this is an illusion?
This time, you know
You've got every question's solution in your head
But the questions aren't the same adding to the confusion

If this was all a dream
Would you enjoy what you dreamt off
Or would it make you scream?

Transport of Delight

There is nothing better than this feeling
And there never will be
When it's just you and those few close friends all together
Reminiscing bad decisions and faint memories

Pictures and videos of night outs
Is all we have left of these times
These memories fade like
The distant sound of wind-struck chimes

There's nothing better than this feeling
And there never will be
The feeling of meeting
Your best mates is ecstasy

Time goes quickly
When you're having a blast
Hours turn to seconds
Damn! Time goes fast

We meet less frequent than we used to
And I blame university for this
But distance can't change the times we've spent together
For these moments replicate eternal bliss

There is nothing better than this feeling
And there never will be
Of how every time we all meet
It leads to a whole new story

I'll say it again because there is nothing better
Than this feeling
And there's no feeling it can't beat
There will be a lot of reeling
When all of us next meet

∽

What If?

As a child I was told
Each step of yours is noted in a book
And at the end of the journey
You'll be questioned for your faults
When you encounter the main attorney

I was naive and young
I was simple and dumb
And pursued a way of life
A bit cautious of what each step could make me become

Eighteen years in and a thought occurred to me
What if this life is only a test?

This seemed too good to be true
Why wouldn't anyone want to live a life
If they are guaranteed not one, but two?
Wouldn't this lead to more destruction and mayhem?
If we all knew this life is only a practise for the real test?
I know I would if I knew I can

The other side of the story occurred to me
This life would lose all its excitement and spontaneity
I would rather live not knowing which path lies ahead
Than living the second life having had all the answers read
Soon, another thought occurred to me

And this is my motto and how I always wanted to be
It nullifies every thought
And erases those words that make us question
What could have become
Of something that is already done

These eleven words are easy to remember
And can be said in a jiff
What would you do if you knew you could not fail?
What if?

We Ought to Have a Longer Weekend

I'm sure I just closed my eyes to sleep
I'm sure this alarm doesn't sound this loud when it beeps

Who's holding down my eyes?
Why does my bed get even more comfy
When it's time to rise?

I'll just put this alarm on snooze
A few minutes of sleep, I can't refuse

Finally! I'm awake
I look at the time
Yet another lecture, I won't be able to make

Who decided on a two-day weekend?
Whoever made this absurd rule
Better step up and make it extend
It's due to these short, two-day breaks
That I wake up missing most Mondays
Tired, and with a headache

All I'm asking for is another day
To help me remember that the weekend is over
And it's getting away

I've come up with a solution and it seems fine to me
I'll count Mondays as off too
And this, I am willing to pretend
Because we ought to have a longer weekend

∽

A Conversation With Myself

I've got my pen, it's full of ink
I sit and wonder what to think
Should I write on terrorism that never seems to stop?
Should I criticize the taxes that shall never drop?

I close my eyes and see myself when I was ten
The younger me starts to speak
He tells me that growing up has turned me into a freak

I answer back, a bit in a daze
I tell him, we all need to grow up and live our life well
He laughs
If this is how you grown-ups live
I rather go to hell
You all get way too serious and think you know it all
And live your life lost in thought, instead of having a ball

This life, it only comes once
And this isn't your permanent address to stay
So grow up if you need to but try and stay young
Because you'll never get a chance to press replay

At this moment, I started to think
That I was going a bit crazy
So I asked him impatiently

Are you for real and why can't I see you?
He said, I'm more realistic than those thoughts
That you worry about
And the only reason you can't see me
Is because you never chose to

I got way too confused and asked him
Why he spoke to me now
He replied
I'm speaking on behalf of every child
That became older
And turned into a bore
Have some fun in life
We didn't grow up to perpetually think of sad times and war

∽

A Moment of Epiphany

There comes a day in everyone's life
When you think of what you've done
There comes a time when you look at your past
And see what you have become

I lie on this bed
Looking at the moments that never say goodbye
I lie waiting for those times to come by
I get out of the bed
That trapped me in my dreams
And I get out of here
So I can become what I should be

So when the time comes
For me to say my final goodbye
I won't regret the moment
And be happy about where I lie

∽

Think Less, Live More

Change, not who you are
But anything negative that you could become
Live life how you want to
Not what you think should be done

Mistakes help us learn lessons
Don't let them become a habit
Live your life cherishing each moment
It's yours, nobody else can grab it

Our biggest enemy is fear
It's a virus that tags along
Stay immune from such problems
Don't let it stop you from being strong

There are no rules to life
But boundaries we should abide
Remember the impact your decisions will make
To those who stand by your side

Think but not too much
It takes a lot of effort and even more time
Be smart and spontaneous
This may seem like an odd mix but trying it isn't a crime
Things happen for a reason

But we decide on what actions we make
So think before each decision you take

Forget the past because it had its chance
Live for today
Before your future slips away

∽

Thank You

I thank you Lord for what I am today
I thank you Lord for leading the way
I thank you Lord but I've got to ask you
What is this life and what is my curfew?

I know this isn't a game, there isn't a pause
And I know there is no audience who will give applause

I wonder and look for a clue
There is no cheat to get me through
There is no button that will make me restart
The only way to complete each level is by being smart
For what we know
We only get one shot
For what we know
This is all we got

I thank you Lord for what I am today
I thank you Lord for leading the way
I've still got something to ask you
Why do we die and why do we kill?
If you won't give me an answer, please give me a clue
Because if there is no solution, there should be a will

Oh Lord, where are you today?
Oh Lord, your creation is going astray
Please give us the guidance we need
Please show us the light
That will help us peacefully breathe

I can't stop thanking you God
But we need to meet
So I can get the answers to all this bloodshed around us

If this life were a game
I know you'd restart
For this world is no old carpet
Which people are tearing apart

The truth is, that there is greed
And I always wonder, what is the need?
I think I know how to succeed in this cruel place
The winner isn't who finishes first or survives till the end
The winner is the one who has the most strength

∽

Politics

From a child:

Why is he wearing such boring clothes?
Why is he speaking Hindi no one knows?
Why do we wait in traffic while they get a clear path?
If these are the perks they get, then even I want to start

From an adult:

I'm not voting for these masses of corruption
Why should I help them fill their pockets
While they cause all this disruption?
Why is he talking about things
That seem like they can't be done?
It's time for the next elections
And his previous promises haven't begun

∽

Roller Coaster of Life

I don't know where this comes from
But there is a moral behind it
Some people say we are here for a reason
The others agree about our fates being decided

We don't know if there's another life
We don't know what happens next
So let's not risk all that's in us
And put our work to the test

Enjoy these moments, not like they're our last
But like many to come with opportunities in store
There are many thoughts to think of
So let your worries affect you no more

I don't know my future and neither do you
Let it be a surprise
And enjoy this moment called the present
It's called 'present' to give us a clue

Learn from your mistakes
And don't let them come in your way
Life is a roller coaster
And it's our personal game to play

∽

The Name Game

What is a name but a mere tag we are born with
Is it an indication of who we ought to be?
What is a name but a path for us to follow
Is it a sign we must see?

We are all born with a name
But it's not who we are
We all live for a certain time but our name stays on
Like a prominent scar

These questions contradict the essence of a name
Whether it is good for one
These questions make me wonder
What the world would be if there were none

The only way its importance is proven,
Is by hearing a name and knowing the deeds it has done
So I lead my life with my surname in mind
So I know the person I need to become

∽

For a Day

If you had the chance to be someone else for a day
Would you want to be an actor winning an Oscar
Or Usain Bolt winning a race?

Would you want to be rich?
Would you want to be known?
Would you want to be someone who is left alone?

We all have our purpose in life
Only a few of us use this opportunity
Would you want to be Gandhi
Achieving freedom for his country?
Or Iniesta scoring the winning goal for Spain's glory?

Life is a stage and we are all performers
If you had the chance
Would you rather be a singer in a big concert?
Or an artist painting his best piece of work?

If I had the choice
I'd want to be the same
Only a bit more focused and in the right lane
We live only once and we can't go astray
I'd want to be the me
I'm dreaming of today

Live Life Well

Look around you, what do you see?
Walls still, wind blowing, people walking
Look inside you, what do you see?
A broken person, a confused soul
Or a happy human being?

Why question ourselves when the answers lie within us?
Why stress ourselves
And not just forget the disasters there are to discuss?

Like there are two sides to a coin, there are to a story
Look at the bright side of life when you face a calamity

What is stress but high blood pressure and more pills?
But what is a smile?
A gesture that takes no skills
Don't be a realist in this pessimistic world
Rather be an optimist and be lazy in bed
Comfortably curled

You'll have to face your troubles
And yes, you'll have to pay your rent
Memories only come from times when you get a dent

You'll be told to sort yourself out
You'll be told you're no good

This life isn't a race
There is no reason why I should
Make others laugh
Make them feel wanted
Being nice won't ever get you taunted

These deeds may lead us to heaven
Or we might just drop into hell
But excuse me, I'm only trying to live this life well

∽

Who Are You?

I look outside and it's bright and sunny
Thinking of you gives shivers in my tummy

I depend on you but you don't depend on me
When I fail you, the pain stings me like a bee

I look outside now and I see the moon
Twelve hours have passed and I've been thinking of you

One more day to meet and I don't know what else to do
I prepare all those lines for our encounter
As it's come way too soon

Who made you and why are you so important to me?
Seriously, who are you?
Even girls think of you and go crazy

We meet today and there's a long list
Only a few minutes to go through the guide books in a jist

Exams, you made me go crazy!
I don't know what to do when you're gone
I find it hard to differentiate noon and dawn
You'll be back to get us all worked up
And pull out our hair

Let me rejoice this time of freedom
Please keep in mind all the thinking of you I did
I hope you get me somewhere

∽

A Dream

I have a dream
Not like what Martin Luther wanted to see
I have a dream
It's pretty big for me

I may not be the hero, I may not be the saviour
But I have a dream
Of seeing every person in the world in their best behaviour

I may seem unrealistic and it may sound weird
This is my dream and to me this isn't absurd

I have a dream
Not like what Gandhi wanted his country to be
I have a dream
To see everyone living together and happy

I know it sounds difficult and stupid
But would this dream be waste to imagine
If I didn't and you did?

I have a dream and I think this one may sound good
I want to live this life being the best I ever could

I have a dream but wait, I think I hear my alarm ringing
I wake up and turn it off
Because I don't want this dream to have an ending

The Road Not Taken

I look through all my messages
And all the people I sent letters to
I look at all those conversations
And promises that were between me and all of you

The things I said, the things I did
Have made me who I am today
The paths I walked, the places I stopped
Will all be gone someday

What remains are the memories of how I've come this far
What is yet to come is my destiny
That could change with each step and each hour

I reminisce about each move of mine
That got me so far from home
I wonder what I would have become if I turned away
Would I still be here on my own?

These questions make me wonder
But they never make me feel mistaken
Of whom I'd be and what I'd be
If I hadn't followed the road not taken

∽

Ready, Set, Go

I was walking down the street,
Loads of people overtaking me
Suddenly I found myself walking faster
And started to see who all I can beat

It made me realise, that we're all athletes
All stuck in one race
All part of one chase
Nobody is going to hesitate
Because everyone wants to hold the fishing rod
Nobody wants to be the bait

We're all climbing the same ladder
Bringing each other down
Trying to reach what will make us happy
Not caring how much this chase makes us frown

We're all slowing down each other's journey
Making it complicated
Only to end up forgetting where we're going
Leaving us frustrated

We're told from the start
That only the one who comes first
Will be remembered
The rest can't be told apart

I guess we're all athletes then
Stuck in this marathon
I'll tie my laces
So I don't get stepped on

∽

Selfish Satisfaction

When this world was made
We didn't have any walls that got us all to separate
We had no obstacles, nothing in between
Everything around us was quaint and green

Now we have hindrances to surpass
Bridges to go across
To go on the other side
Which is now just burnt down grass

I don't blame religion
I don't blame cultures
It's us humans, who are to blame
All we want is power and pride
When peace and tranquillity should be our primary aim

No one ever differentiated between one another
Now it's only people from one religion
Who you can call your brother
This world wasn't made to be broken into different parts
All this bloodshed and war
Has only led to losing lives and breaking hearts

We fight to attain peace
But nobody realises the irony of their action

Soon this earth will be a blood-filled war land
Only because we can't achieve our selfish satisfaction

∽

Nobody Cares

Nobody knows
Nobody cares
All I get is abuse and stares

Nobody asks me, what I feel
They all just act like they know the deal
But I'm just like a book
And all they've read is the cover
Nobody cares whether I'll recover

Just because I sit here
Just because I don't speak
They all judge me
Instead of wondering why I'm weak

I can hear them talk
Although behind my back
Their abuse is as often as the seconds on a clock

They still don't know
They still don't care
They all make up their own story to share

I'll let them win
I'll keep them guessing
Their teasing is the worst sin

So, alas, they win
And I'll permanently get rid of this misery
Maybe what I need is a new place to begin

Hopefully one day they'll know
The reason for my state was their judgement and abuse
Maybe one day they'll see that I didn't fall off the edge
It was they who pushed me

ᔓ

Dear Government

Excuse me, can I have some thread
To sew this hole in my pocket please?
How did it happen?
Oh, actually the government isn't aware
That money doesn't grow on trees

I'm not being dramatic!
The petrol price rise is burning us down
So much for our country being democratic

At least the government is getting rid of poverty
As they said they would
Never realised they'd do it
By getting rid of the poor by increasing prices
I think we all misunderstood

Dear government, we're 'glad' our taxes help you get richer
But can we get rid of some corruption a bit quicker?

Why is it harder to get admission in school?
And so expensive to buy fuel?
Whereas, getting away with speeding and rash driving
Is a cake walk
I'm starting to believe
Your speeches at the time of elections
Are nothing but talk

I wish the public had a choice at the time of election
Because if we vote you out
We're voting in your mirror reflection!

∽

Nation at Stake

I'm forever harping about corruption
I tend to forget those
Who are trying to get rid of this disruption

It takes one to lead and we have 1.2 billion leaders in us
We all need to get together to get rid of this fuss

The country isn't corrupt, only a few people are
But there are people, who are all ready to help
They just get overshadowed by those with wealth
Because it doesn't help that the main authority is corrupt
Not realising that their actions
Are causing the nation to erupt

We are continuously told
That in ten years we're going to be a super power
But with this menace
That time is extending with each minute, each hour
It's time for all of us to awake
Because this is our nation at stake

∽

Customer We Care

'Your call is important to us, please stay on the line'
Five minutes later, I'm sitting at the same place
Listening to the same recording on the phone
Trying to solve the problem I called for, on my own

Why are you called customer care?
Were you trying to be ironic?
If not, why don't you answer the phone
And help when we call you
If you have any time to spare?

You put us on hold
When you should answer our question
Let us know you can't help when we call
Instead of wasting our time
That's my suggestion

Customer we care when we want to
Is an apt name for you
Next time I call
Stop putting me on hold
And help me with the solutions that I called to be told

∽

Déjà Vu

Didn't I just walk past this street?
Or is this déjà vu?
Although this place is completely new
Lately my actions cause my heart to skip a beat

No one knows me in this new place
But each person I look at has a familiar face
Maybe I've come here
Or maybe they live near

Lately every action seems to have happened before
As if I have already walked through each door
As if my script was a book I wrote
As if someone is pressing repeat from the remote

Am I still sane?
Maybe questioning that factor does state
That there are a few flaws in my brain
Yet they seem like I've seen them before in a dream
But why do only a few occur
While the rest seem to have evaporated like steam

It's clear now
At least this seems like the only justification
To prove that I'm not insane

Our life is previewed by us when we are born
We choose to forget what we want
So the rest of the action we call déjà vu
Is in fact our future we've stored in our brain

∽

Every Moment

With each step forward
I move closer to the finish line
The same way you get closer to finishing a book
With each word read

With each action, I form my own destiny
The same way each drop of water forms the sea
Unlike a film, my life has no reel to look back
Neither can I retake my past, as if it were an exam

With each day that goes by
I've either moved forward or remained where I was
As if stuck on standby
I guess, it's up to us to decide whether we like it or not
So, with every second
It's up to us to make use of what we've got

∽

Farewell

When you have fun, time flies
And now that I think about the times we all shared
It's hard to say my goodbyes
I'll see you all, at least I hope I do
It's obvious I'll miss your faces
And I hope you all miss me too

Two years went by too fast
I arrived scared, oblivious to what lies ahead of me
But it all got overshadowed by the journey
That I was yet to see
All those joyous times
Are now merely memories from the past

I guess what they say is true
When you're having fun
Time doesn't wait for you
And that's exactly my case
The journey has gone past in the quickest pace

So, as I walk out of these doors for the last time
Memories rush through my head like a mime
These last two years of school feel too good to be true
And it wouldn't have been possible
If it wasn't for you

God's Best Friend

When I was born
I was confused on who you were
And why you seemed so surreal
But to the word perfect, you're ideal

Whenever I came home crying or acted like a brat
You changed the emotions to happiness and
Whatever the mess might be
Got it intact

With time to come
I grew older and tall
But whenever you'd take care of me
I'd go back to being carefree and small

I often wondered how you were always so calm
And cheered me up in every moment we would spend
I've started to realise you're God's best friend

I know it's true
And you strengthen the reasons with everything you do
Because mom, with every moment we spend
I can't thank you enough for also being my best friend

∽

I Don't Want to Grow Up

I couldn't stand waking up so early, at six
I didn't understand why my bag was so heavy
I often contemplated whether my books were actually bricks

The same old routine
The same old canteen
I never understood why they said
School was the house of education
I still can't differentiate
Between Algebra and regular calculation

The senior years made school seem like a joy to attend
Attending classes became an occasion
Bunking, a common trend

The canteen became the new hang out
The basket ball court the new hiding spot
Only post exams would I regret
Not listening to what we were taught

Those days now seem like a distant memory of some sort
Life seems much more serious and unorganised
I wish I could still run and find my friends
Sitting by the basketball court

The alarm ringing at early hours seem like a passing sound
I wish I could go back to the school field
And press pause when I was at the ground

School did teach me one thing that will stay on forever
The feeling of nostalgia
When I look back to those five days in a week
I can recall some memories as if they were a video
With each action and each word my friends would speak

I don't get why school was so much fun
Maybe I didn't use it the right way
No work, only play
But if I had the chance, I would relive each day
With no change, skipping the same lessons
Running from teachers, the same way

I wish I was Peter Pan
Not having to grow older, always staying young
If I had the chance, I'd go back to school whenever I can
So I could go back to the time
I learnt to use a beaker and a measuring cup
Because I don't want to grow up

∽

If There Was No Tomorrow

If there was no tomorrow
I wouldn't be sad
And I wouldn't show any signs of sorrow
Instead I'll be happy and I'll be glad
Because I've lived every moment
Better than I could have

I won't hope for a time machine
I won't hope for a miracle to take me back in time
Instead I'll be happy about where I am
Still knowing there was more I could climb

This life only gives us our starting date
And keeps the end as a surprise
So it's up to us to make sure our job is done
When the end date arrives

The end is only a rough deadline
To fulfil all that you want to
So I'll take this date to be a gift
Because if there is no tomorrow
I'll be ready, having done all that I wanted to do
Because life isn't about what you couldn't do so far
It's about what you have done
The journey isn't about reaching your goal quickly
It's about how those miles were run

Journey

This is my story
Don't tell me the end
This isn't all about glory
So just let it flow my friend

I'm not going to brake
Whatever might be at stake
I'm not afraid to go
Wherever the wind may blow
And I won't hesitate
Whatever be my fate

This is my story
And there's much more to be done
I've just begun

I'm here to give it all
And I'm here to have a ball
Because I'm far from the end
And whatever be the journey, I won't apprehend

I'm not going to look behind
You're free to sit by my side
And we can all lose our mind
Because it's all about enjoying the ride

This is my story
And it's still incomplete
I've got loads to prove and loads to show
So I'm going to go ahead now
And enjoy where this journey is going to make me go

ᔕ

Just Do It

Do what you want to do
Only being a dreamer won't make your dreams come true
It's like Nike says 'Just do it'
So don't just talk about your goals
Get yourself into it!

You can either sit there
And dream about reaching your goal
Or you can get up and do the main role
Because only after sleepless nights
Do you get a good night in
So don't waste your time
Get up and let your journey begin!

∽

Letter to God

Letter from a rich kid to God:
I didn't like the remote control car I got last time
It wasn't fast enough and all my friends had it
Now I play tennis, so I want Federer's racket

Letter from a poor kid to God:
I've heard you can do anything
But I don't want any gift
I only wish to get rid of all this suffering
I don't want to seem too needy
But can you make the walk to get clean water closer?
I hope I'm not sounding too greedy
Also, I've been told my friends have gone away
I haven't been told but I know they died of hunger
And I know asking to feed us all will be too much
But please make us stronger
I thank you for what I have
And I thank you for all that you've done
If you ever need to find me
I'll be the one finding water for my family
Under this scorching sun

The rich kid got what he wanted and much more
The other one succumbed to the sun
You might think the rich kid had better luck

But he still wasn't content with all that he had
On the outside he was happy but forever lived sad
Because money couldn't buy him everything
So he lived his whole materialistic life with a fake smile
The latter didn't have to live longer in that state
He wasn't ignored and forgotten
He met his lost friends and family
At the entry of heaven's gate

Anything You'd Like to Call It

I don't know what it was back then
We were at an age when the opposite sex didn't relate
But I still hid all my stationary just to borrow your pen
Maybe I was too young then to put it straight
But, talking to you gave me something like a sugar rush
I guess I can admit, you were my first crush

I can remember enough memories to write an essay
But I won't recognise you now when you cross my way
So I'll take that time to be an important phase
When instead of just sports, I had another craze

I wonder now, if you felt the same
But then I wonder if you even remember my name
Back then I did go out of my way to get your attention
Skipping games period once almost got me detention!

Looking back now makes me realise
Why this crush faded away
My best friend liked you too
And you seemed to come in our friendship's way
So I guess it's fair to assess
The norm back then was more important to me
Than us to progress

∽

Deadlines

If there weren't any deadlines
Would you wait to do your work till eternity?
Ah! What an easy life that would be

What if your exams never had a time limit?
You could keep attempting them till you wanted
Never having to give up and quit

I don't like the word deadline
It gives shivers down my spine
Makes me think of something still
As if the only way from here is downhill

But maybe we need a time limit
To all that we do
But just like we know the end time to all exams
And the sports we play
Wouldn't you want to know the time you have to go?
So you can do all that you want while you stay

∽

A Year Has Gone By

It's been a year since you've gone
This hide and seek game has been on far too long
I've been waiting at the same place for a while
I want to hear your voice on the other end when I dial

Have things been the same?
Have we been fine?
If we haven't, who do we blame?
We've all been strong, I've tried too
You've been up there looking down on us
And there hasn't been a single day
Where we haven't missed you

I'm turning twenty *dadi*!
I won't drop anything on the floor, at least I'll try not to
Please come and wish me *dadi*
I don't like this distance between me and you

I'm sorry I wasn't around much
I was busy trying to make a name
Gift me a remote *dadi*
So I can rewind to one of our card games

I'm looking around now
Hoping to hear a whisper or any proof of you around
Please give me a sign or make a sound

I know you're by my side
And always will be
So every time anything fun happens
It's a laugh for both you and me

Thank you for the strength *dadi*
But can you please come and wish me
Please give me your address *dadi*
I'll come wherever you will be

∽

Non Sibi Sed Omnibus

With the help of others we learn how to speak
When we come into this world
Without them we would remain quiet and curled

We need others' assistance
For our own existence
We need to offer our hand
To help others stand

We aren't a part of a competition
We all need to form a coalition
Because coming together is a beginning
Keeping together is progress
And working together is success

Non sibi sed omnibus
Should be the way ahead
Oh, how different this world would be
If unity was widespread

∽

Parallel Universe

What is this place?
Why are happiness and unity the only themes?
This is just like the place the whole world hopes for
In their dreams!

Maybe I am asleep
I guess, I'll just wait for my alarm to beep
Till then, I'll stroll down these absurd lanes
Everything seems intact
No sound of guns, no sight of blood stains

I see people of all races playing in the park
No line of borders, no sight of the dark
I hear screams!
At last evidence that this place isn't as surreal as it seems
I follow the noise
Only to realise I enter a room filled with laughter and joys

I don't fit in here
For a person coming from where I live
I can only be a sight seer

I finally see a sign
Which makes me realise why according to earth
Everything here is inverse

It reads out with a halo-like light around it
'Welcome to the Parallel Universe'

ᔕ

Pencil Full of 'Lead'

I thought it was all coming to an end
In a few hours, I'd be no more, dead!
I should have been careful
It wasn't wise to have rested my hand
Onto a sharpened pencil's lead

Who sharpened the pencil similar to a knife?
The lead in me was taking away my right to life

Maybe I got a bit over dramatic
But my friends told me the lead is poisonous
As a twelve-year old
The news for me was quite traumatic

I was told to drink lots of water
And put my hand in the freezer
I listened to my friends' advice
Submerged my hand in a bucket of ice
I was informed only after a fortnight
That nothing would have happened to me
And I didn't need any aid
This was a prank the two played
Only then did I learn
Pencils don't have lead in them, it's merely graphite!

Saturday Encounters

What would you do if you knew there was no tomorrow?
Every time before those horrid encounters
Which were full of sorrow
I'd live the day before doing all that I wanted
Just in case I didn't make it through

Oh, how I remember those meetings
If words could be put into action
I endured quite a few beatings

I'll admit, I was at fault too
But I think my actions were over exaggerated when told
After all, I was only a child, what else was I to do?
Oh, how I wish, that excuse was sold!

I usually looked forward to the weekend
But a week before those terrifying Saturday encounters
I'd be in my room
Scared yet knowing what I'd have to attend

Their words didn't make much of a difference to me
Call me a menace
But if they could expand one fault of mine into two
I would help them increase that tally to three

But then the cycle would continue to go on
I'd know what lies ahead
But I'd still wish I could skip those encounters at dawn

I'm glad that episode in my life is over
Well, at least that's what I pray
Because I'm still terrified of attending another PTA!

∽

Rebel Without a Cause

You look at me
You look at us
While sitting in your bullet proof cars
While we're pushing for space in this broken down bus

I find it funny
How you judge us
Call us names, stereotype as being illiterate
Not knowing why we make a fuss

Oh please, Mr I'm-so-rich, Mrs perfect
But we'll be kind to you
If you give us reasons to earn our respect

We lost one of our people today
Don't worry, loads more have joined us
I guess they prefer our way

This system causes so many to die of hunger and poverty
It makes us sick
That you're walking around unaffected and free

So next time you look at us
Before judging me and my people while we're on the bus
Why don't you see your own flaws
Maybe then you'll realise, we aren't rebels with no cause

Living Shadow

I look at you and I see a reflection
I look at you but there's a disconnection
So I get out and face the rain
Looking at you smiling while you hide your tears and pain
I try to see me in you
While I stand there feeling blue
Knowing there's not much you can do

I run through my day in my head
I wasted every minute, every hour
All those tasks I planned to do
Were left undone, only said

I think back to the boy on the road
What would he have done if he was in my place?
Would he let any opportunity erode?

I guess this world is an evil place
Those who are gifted with opportunities
Let them pass with a straight face
While our reflections who we look at from our window
Don't get a chance to get on the other side of the door
And end up living as our shadow

Steps to Learn How to Drive

I was excited, a bit nervous too
But if driving was as easy as the games in the arcade
I knew I'll be able to drive in a day or two

To my disappointment, I was mistaken
After seeing the chaos on the road
It didn't seem the same
I contemplated a couple of times
Whether to go back to driving in those fictional games

On my first day of class
I drove on a computer screen
A bit too easy, I think I knew I'd pass

The second day came as a shock
My instructor came to pick me up
Speeding at me, on the phone
Oblivious to the concept of a seat belt
Suddenly my confidence shattered as if hit by a rock

I'll never forget his 'inspiring' words
'Think for yourself, everyone else on the road is a fool'
At first his words felt a bit ironic and absurd
But as I got on to the road
It seemed like an overcrowded pool

Ever walked on a treadmill?
Where you're at the same place
Although you feel you're moving ahead
That's the same feeling on the road
Sometimes while you see the other cars moving forward
Brake is the only pedal that can be pressed

I'll admit, it took a lot of courage to go behind the wheel
So I think twice before I drive an automobile
'Because everyone else on the road is a fool'
How I wish I actually passed the driving school!

∽

System

'Life is unfair'
Fight your own battles
I grew up to this motto as if it were a lullaby
Instead of spreading happiness in my family
I was born as a burden and only made them sigh

At the age of eight
I was shining shoes for the rich
Who I'd already started to hate

Money wasn't a problem in the household
But that's because it would never stay
All the money we'd earn, by the night would be spent
On one measly meal before the following day

Luck did come our way
At least that's what I would say
Shining shoes earned me a job at a factory to bottle booze
Sufficient money was finally being earned
A commodity my family forever had yearned

A rainbow only comes after a spell of rain
So once this rainbow vanished
My illiteracy caused me a lot of pain

Industrialisation made its arrival
I lost my job along with many more
Who were fighting for their survival

What was I to do?
The same bottles of booze I manufactured
Became my only friend
I blame this system for my illiteracy and my end

∽

Masses of Destruction

Why should you get a place to stay?
When grief and pain is all that you give
And the rest of the world to you is nothing but a prey

Why can't you face us?
Why do you hide?
Why are fear and anger
Messages that you spread worldwide?

Let's not blame religion
Let's keep aside corruption too
How about you explain the reason for this destruction
Which you keep adding to?

What did that cyclist do to you?
Or the group of children from junior high?
I don't think you could hear their cries while you hid
But what did they do, to deserve to die?

I bet you love being associated with terror
I mean all the offence when I say
You're the strongest connotation to an error

How about you stop hiding and face us all
Remember the world is a big place

And there are only a minute number of you
So you should know who's going to be the one standing tall

If words could get through to you at all
I'll suggest you forget all this bloodshed and brawl
Because we live once and this is the only chance we get
So I rather live it without living under a continuous threat

The Only Certainty

There is only one certainty in life
That is death and being no more
But why is there no strength in us when we lose someone
Even though we know of this sin from before

There is no reason for the end
Is there no way to extend this date?
Or act like it's not happened and just pretend?

Just like the finish line in a race
Our loved ones have to end their time
Leaving behind memories
That play often like a wind-struck chime

Maybe they go because this world is of no good
They leave for a better place
I guess this concept of death has been misunderstood

Or maybe they leave to welcome those they love
Maintaining the quaint and surreal environment above

I guess, they leave
Because an empty house, no one appreciates
So when our time comes
We'll be welcomed by our loved ones, at heaven's gate

The Real Sin

They were fated to pretend
Only till the end
When they realised that this is only the starting line
Nobody knew where to begin
Only wanting to win
Didn't get them very far

With no aim in their head
Only wanting to succeed
Made them as good as dead
With no directions in mind
Walking as if they were blind
Didn't help them proceed

They were all hypnotised by one sin
Although realising within
They let the demon take the lead
Learning the hard way
By ending up lost and astray
They all gave up the sin, the drug, their greed

∽

The Test

It's like you're speaking to someone
But there is no one else near you
It's like you're trying to shout
But the words aren't getting through

It's like I'm walking on a treadmill
I'm still
A bit like, walking in the opposite direction on an escalator
I try so hard to get across to everyone
But I don't make sense
It's like I need a translator

I often think of the easy way out
Give up and have nothing to think about
But then this feeling in me
I think they call it guilt
Starts to drill sense in me
Now I get why it's inbuilt

So I get back up and I fall back down
I keep going and never drown
Because the only way forward is by learning how to fall
Just like it takes one shot at a time to break a wall

So I look back now
And see where I am
Thinking of the obstacles that came my way
And caused a traffic jam
Hindrances are important
To make the journey to success worthwhile
Just so the race to the finish line is challenging at each mile

∽

A Voice Within

It's like your shadow that never leaves you alone
It's like your soul
Something that is attached to each part of your body
Each muscle, each bone

But what is this thought?
Why does it not go away?
Is it a message from within?
If so, what is it trying to say?

These thoughts, they never leave me alone
Always there like a friend in need
Maybe it's a voice in us
Pushing us to succeed

It's like we're stuck in a tunnel and
Our thoughts are the light
It's like we're blind
And these thoughts give us sight

These thoughts are the path that leads the way
In the smooth journeys and during the rough terrains
These thoughts will never let me go astray

∽

A Toast to Life

Picture the moment
People are gathered all together
All those with whom your life was spent
Would you want them gloomy
Having nothing to say about you?
Or would you want them toasting with champagne
Because your life left a mark as if it were a permanent tattoo?

Our life is a message to the rest
Live it such, that everyone knows what you did
As if they were answers to a test

Wouldn't you rather end on a happy note?
Not leaving any chapter unread
Knowing that you don't need to row any further
And you can finally park your boat

I'd rather that day be a happy event
So, I'll live my life like a dream
And hope to leave my mark
As if it were embedded with cement

∽

Unsung Heroes

Nobody appreciates the dark
They praise the light
The dark is where they sleep and get respite

No one ever spoke of the field
Everyone just praised the game
But did you even once think
Without the ground, it wouldn't have been the same?

There are people like this
For us they are nothing but a shadow
Without them life wouldn't be easy
They are like a tap, that helps water flow
Like the wheels to a car that get unnoticed

Just like each pillar is important to hold a building
Without these people our world would sink

To you they are just a shadow
Who you'll never know
But for me, they are the unsung heroes

∽

Key to Destiny

The roof seems to cave in
It's time to begin
But my feet don't move
I'm stuck to the ground
Despite knowing where I'm bound

The walls are closing down on me
It's getting harder to breathe
I need to find the key
Unlock and walk down the road
To where I'm meant to be
To call it my destiny

∽

Carry On

They say that life is a race
I'll get left behind
If I don't keep up with the pace

It took years for me to realise
The importance of that statement
My views and goals changed along with the development

Sitting and relaxing was how my holidays were spent
Now it seems a waste of time
Something holding me back from being content

If I stop moving ahead
Instead of being a leader
I'll start being led
Because this world is a track
And we are running a race
Stuck in a never ending chase

∽

A Spark

Everyone needs inspiration
A light that guides you home
Everyone needs exhilaration
An adrenaline rush
That flows between each muscle and bone

Some follow their idols
Others' journey flows like a stream
I get inspired from my goal
Since I wake, till it's my dream

We need motivation to cover the journey
We need a spark to ignite the fire within
A kick start and our journey begins

Some come to lead
Others to follow
Reminiscing each moment and enjoying each step
The memories I make for tomorrow

Looking for inspiration
Seeking motivation
Looking back at the first step since I chose to begin
Realising I don't need to look further
My journey is enough to push me forward
Inspiring me from within

That Bond

Like a watch
With each second that ticks away
The time changes
The hands rotate in the same manner with each hour
With each day

Where is the generation gap?
Is it in the pictures that aren't just black and white?
Or is it because we're in different places on the map?
Nothing seems to differentiate us
When I look through these old snaps

One thing that makes us all the same
Despite the generations between us
We're all held together by a single bond
A bond, as strong and valuable as a diamond
That bond, being nothing other than our name

I sit looking at this picture of my family tree
The generation maybe different
But a gap between them?
I wouldn't agree

I stare at these pictures only to see
The reason there is no gap is
These generations have combined, to make me

Fear and Failure

In life, hindrances will come your way
Scars will be a reminder of your falls and will always stay
But it's not about how hard you fall
Or how many times you lose
Life is about how you overcome those times
When you felt blue

During your journey
You might lose your way
You might feel like you've gone astray
Only when we fall down
Do we need to make the effort to get back to our feet
Take every failure in your stride
They occur to make us stronger, not to cause our defeat

Our biggest failures occur due to fear
The fear to do something new
We might fail when we try
But if we never attempt
We'll never know, how we would do

Failure isn't the end
It's proof that you have tried
Failure is a friend
Like a light showing us the path to success
Always acting as a guide

Born For a Purpose

We're born writers
We're born with a pen
Writers of our fate
Of the journey that lies ahead of us
We come up with anything we want to create

We're born for a purpose
Some live their lives finding answers
Others forget the questions
And focus on their progression

We're born discoverers
Searching an aim
Finding motivation
To ignite the flame

We're born to die
We're all born to last
Some get forgotten with time
Others are considered a blast from the past

∽

30 Seconds of Fame

I have this theory
It's a bit of a cliché
We're all here to perform
But we only get the stage for 30 seconds
To showcase ourselves in our own unique way

That's where the difference can be seen
Between those that remain where they are
While, a few move up
Springing off a trampoline

We all get our time to shine
We all get our spot under the limelight
It depends on how we perform
We can either earn a standing ovation
Or a get a stage fright

We're all here for a reason
Some spend their time finding the meaning
The other use these 30 seconds over and over again
To achieve all that they are dreaming
Whoever makes use of their 30 seconds
Their time will extend
If you perform all the way through
The stage is yours till the end

Summer Exit

Summer has come to an end
Never realised when time started to descend
We're all packing and leaving to continue our journey
Getting back in the mind set to reach our dream
We'll be thousands of miles away
But we'll always be a team

Never understood this time of the year
We've spent months together
The time moved at the speed of light
Soon enough, we shall be back on our own
And those memories will seem like a distant sight

Winter is the next time we all meet
But three months seem way too much
There needs to be a way to pass this time quicker
An alteration, maybe even a cheat?

Summer has made its exit and gone
We've parted our ways
The things said, the times shared stick on
For something good, you have to wait
I'll reminisce the memories in store till the due date

∽

Summer Promises

Four months, over a hundred days
I know promises shouldn't be broken
But I've broken more than I can count, in many ways

Summer was long awaited
'Time to get your act together, Sanil
Make use of these days, don't let them go waste'
Summer came to an end
Regardless of my 'motivational speech'
No action was generated!

I blame the heat for this lacks behaviour
Oh wait, I used that last summer
I'll just say summer wasn't the right season
The winter break will be my saviour

I didn't get in shape
Didn't earn any money
I blame you, Summer
Why do you have to be so relaxed and sunny?!

A few summer promises added to the list
If these goals aren't lost in the winter mist
Summer, I guess it'll be till next time we meet
Hopefully, these promises, won't fade away in your heat

Stay Alert, Stay Bright!

Look left, look right
Stay alert, stay bright!
This is no longer a safe place
Everyone's busy in their own chase
Each to their own
Everyone for themselves

Look left, look right
Stay alert, stay bright!
This world is an arena where all we do is fight
But nothing can fill the greedy man's plight

It's called the human race for a reason
Everyone is in the chase to get to the top
Whatever may be the season

Stay awake and stay alert
If you aren't a part of this system
You might get hurt
Corruption and crime are the way ahead
'It's a free world' someone once said
Doesn't seem like that now
We're back to war and bloodshed

Where is Life Taking Me?

Humans are funny species
We take credit for all that we have done
We blame our destiny for our misfortune
From the time it begun

We question, where we are
We blame our failure
On our horoscope or the movement of each star

Do we ever look back to see how far have we come?
Has life got us here?
Who has got us to do, all that we have done?

We wonder where we are
Only to realise the progress we have made to come so far
Where was I and where is life taking me?
Or am I the sailor of my own ship?
Sailing, however rough the sea might be?

'Where is life taking me?'
Sounds like a mistake
Knowing that I'm leading my life
Makes me feel stronger, makes me feel awake!

∽

Play the Game

You have to play the game to succeed
Only by trying will you know if you'd lose
Or be in the lead

Beat your fear
It's the biggest obstacle that can come your way
Challenge yourself
It'll make you stronger with each day

We're all part of a game
From the time we are born
Make the most of this opportunity
Be the one who sets the norm

Do so well in the game
That everybody knows your name
If you don't try
You'll never know
Whether you'd stay where you were
Or how far you could go

Be a part of the game
Be the one who succeeds
Because if you want to hear the echo of your name
You'll need to be the one who leads

Looking Back

Looking back at the times
When I was a child
Whatever used to happen
I would be satisfied

Take me back to those days
Take me back to those ways
When life was more than just about money
And being high in society

Looking back at those years
I did all that I wanted to
Only because I didn't know the meaning of fear

Take me back
And let me stay
Take me back
And let those times take over from the ones today
We're all puppets
And our modern thoughts, the puppeteer
So, let's forget this materialistic way of life
And get that way of living, back here

∽

Life on Mars

Technology has the solutions to many questions
That are now answered
We can talk to people living far away
If that's not enough
We now have an eye on Mars
If there is life present there
If there ever will be, some day

For other existence we seem to care
But when it comes to one's self
Our concern gets lost in this polluted air
We're so busy trying to intrude on others' lives

I'm proud of all this progression
But where is the money for the poor and needy
Then we say we're in severe recession

I wish I could send a message
To whoever we find on Mars
If you can hear me
I warn you not to come to this unfair planet
You're better off staying in space next to the stars
And I apologise on behalf of this society
For this intrusive act of ours

I hope we find someone there
Something like a parallel universe
Where instead of bloodshed and corruption
We can learn how to live together and care

Acknowledgements

Just like a building needs support of every pillar to stand up straight, I wouldn't have been able to gain the courage to pen down my thoughts, if it wasn't for my pillars of strength, my family. I would also like to thank all those people, whom I have encountered and personally know, for playing an important role in shaping me into the individual I am today and into the person reflected in this book.

∽

www.ingramcontent.com/pod-product-compliance
Lightning Source LLC
LaVergne TN
LVHW091007080826
845145LV00003B/1167